YOUR KNOWLEDGE HAS VALUE

- We will publish your bachelor's and master's thesis, essays and papers

- Your own eBook and book - sold worldwide in all relevant shops

- Earn money with each sale

Upload your text at www.GRIN.com
and publish for free

Dave Ray

Business Deconstructed - Games Workshop

GRIN Verlag

Bibliografische Information der Deutschen Nationalbibliothek:

Die Deutsche Bibliothek verzeichnet diese Publikation in der Deutschen National-
bibliografie; detaillierte bibliografische Daten sind im Internet über http://dnb.d-
nb.de/ abrufbar.

Imprint:

Copyright © 2012 GRIN Verlag GmbH
Druck und Bindung: Books on Demand GmbH, Norderstedt Germany
ISBN: 978-3-656-35876-3

This book at GRIN:

http://www.grin.com/en/e-book/208292/business-deconstructed-games-workshop

GRIN - Your knowledge has value

Der GRIN Verlag publiziert seit 1998 wissenschaftliche Arbeiten von Studenten, Hochschullehrern und anderen Akademikern als eBook und gedrucktes Buch. Die Verlagswebsite www.grin.com ist die ideale Plattform zur Veröffentlichung von Hausarbeiten, Abschlussarbeiten, wissenschaftlichen Aufsätzen, Dissertationen und Fachbüchern.

Visit us on the internet:

http://www.grin.com/

http://www.facebook.com/grincom

http://www.twitter.com/grin_com

Business Deconstructed

Dave Ray

2012

Word Count: 3299

New College Durham

Contents

Introduction

Company Profile

For the assignment the report will be evaluating the British company Games Workshop Group PLC. The Games Workshop principle activities are the design, manufacture and retail of miniature figures, metal soldiers and rulebooks. It offers its products under Warhammer and Warhammer 40,000 brands and operates in the UK, USA, Canada, France, Germany Spain, Italy, Japan and Australia. It is headquartered in Nottingham, the UK and employs around 2,066 people.

The business was founded in in 1975 and was originally a manufacturer of wooden board games and later became an importer of the *Dungeons & Dragons* role playing game from the United States and expanded from a mail order company to opening its own retail shop in 1979. The company continued its growth in the 80's and 90's and floated on the London Stock Exchange in October 1994. In 2011 Games Workshop reported a turnover of £123,100,000

The assignment is looking at how legal form determines the company's relationship with the stakeholders. To do this effectively the report will look at what legal form is and what shareholders are?

Legal Form

There are various legal forms in Business which can be seen in the following table and also gives a brief description of advantages and disadvantages of each

Legal Form	Description	Advantages	Disadvantages
Sole Trader	Sole Traders are essentially *the business*. Legally the business and the person are the same, which means that they are responsible for debts and taxes	Very Easy to start a Sole Trader Business and very little paperwork involved	The owner is liable for the business and any debts or leases pertaining the business
Partnership	Partnerships are set up by a Deed of Partnership and witnessed by a solicitor. The deed sets up legal relationship and sets how profits are divided as well as responsibilities.	Businesses can come together in a partnership or a business can be started by two people. Liability of a business can be divided by the partners	Partners are liable for debts and leases similar to Sole Trader. Partnerships may not work out because of personal problems
Private Limited Company	Private Limited Companies are legally separate from their owners. The shareholders are usually the owners	Private limited companies' shareholders are not liable for the company's debts and responsibilities	The paperwork is more complex than the previous legal forms.
Public Limited Company	Public Limited companies are a limited liability company that sells shares to the public	Limited Liability, Separate entity and Taxation and Tax Advantages	Complex accounts along with restricted capital raising and dilutions of powers

Games Workshop Group plc is a public limited company. Public Limited companies can offer shares of the company for sale to the public as stated by the UK Companies Act 1980. For a business to be a public liability company, the business must have *plc* at the end of the name and must register with Companies House which is an Executive Agency of the Department for Business. For a business to be formed as a plc it must have

- A certificate of entitlement to do business and borrow capital
- A minimum of £50,000 of share capital, of which 25% must have been paid for.
- Two directors, one of whom may be the company secretary.
- Two shareholders
- Section 86 of the Companies Act 2006 requires all plc's to have registered address

Clayton (2008) states that a limited company as

> *"A 'separate legal identity'. Profits and losses are the company's and has its own debts and obligations. The business continues despite the resignation, death or bankruptcy of management and shareholders and it offers the ideal vehicle for expansion and the participation of outside investors."*

Clayton writes that a public limited company is the *"the ideal vehicle for expansion"* and this refers to a plc offering shares for sales to the public. Companies can do this to generate money for the business to possibly invest or expand, and in return a percentage is paid to the shareholder in a dividend[1]

Advantages and Disadvantages of a Public Limited company

Bové et al (2005) writes that the main advantage of a public limited company is that it has unlimited capital available to them through the investment from shareholders. This gives a public limited company the opportunity to invest in marketing, development or expansion easier than a private organisation due to access of capital. This investment by shareholders also means that the shareholders have a vested interest in the business, and with this comes a responsibility of the business to the shareholders as well. Also as there are shareholders to take into consideration, this could hold back a business from being more *revolutionary* due to financial risks and also shareholders may not want to take risky business decisions as it may affect their share value. These reasons are the disadvantages of a plc.

This section has touched upon *shareholders*, and the next section goes into detail about what they are.

Shareholders

The assignment brief asks how the company's legal form determines the organisations relationship with its stakeholders (the emphasis should be on the investor stakeholder group. Figure 1 shows who the stakeholders are in the Games Workshop Group plc.

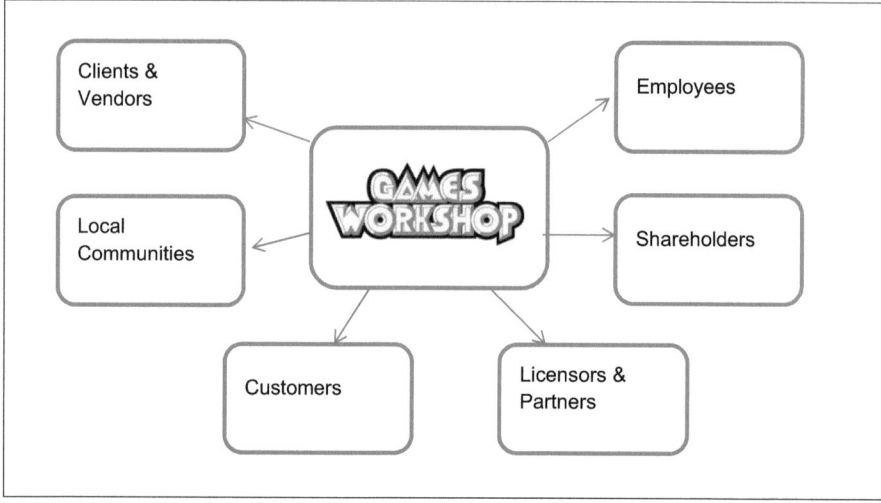

As the assignment has specifically identified the **investor** stakeholder group, the report will look at the relationship between the two.

Shareholders (or stockholders[2]) have been defined by William (2005, p179) as

> "people who own a coprporations stock- and thus own part of the corporation – are called stockholders or sometimes **shareholders**. Once a corporation has been formed, it may sell its shares to individuals or other companies that want to invest in the corporation. It also may issue stock as a reward to key employees in return for services."

People who invest into a business would do so by purchasing shares in the company, and for this investment the person becomes a shareholder and, if the company creates a profit, the shareholder is entitled to a part of the profit called a dividend. With this in mind, the shareholder has a vested interest in the company, and for the business to be run in a manner that protects the shareholders' investment, shareholders vote for a 'director' who would be responsible for the everyday running of the company. (Dine, 1994)

Company/Shareholder Relationship

The relationship between the shareholder and the company is controlled by Corporate Governance and is a way of protecting the shareholders interest. This is done by enabling shareholders to

- ✓ Secure methods of ownership registration
- ✓ Transfer shares
- ✓ Obtain information on the corporation
- ✓ Participate and vote in shareholder meetings
- ✓ Elect members of the board
- ✓ Share in the profits of the company.

(Tricker, 2003)

The annual report of the Games Workshop Group plc stipulates on page 15 that

> *"The Listing Rules of the Financial Services Authority require listed companies to disclose, in relation to section 1 of the June 2008 Combined Code on Corporate Governance (the Combined Code), how they have applied its principles and whether they have complied with its provisions throughout the accounting period. The Combined Code can be found at http://www.frc.org.uk.*
>
> *This statement, together with the remuneration report on pages 19 to 22, explains how the Company has applied the principles and complied with the provisions set out in the Code."*

The annual report also informs the reader that the board operates through monthly meetings, however the Companies Act 2006, section 336 stipulates

> *"Every public company must hold a general meeting as its annual general meeting in each period of 6 months beginning with the day following its accounting reference date"*

http://www.legislation.gov.uk/ukpga/2006/46/section/336

The annual report is to ensure that all shareholders are aware of how the company is performing.

The Annual Report also offers information to prospective investors with the figures from the balance sheet; however investors would look at specifically at the Independent Auditors Report. This report gives information on the validity of the annual reports results and this can be found on page 25. For the Games Workshop Group plc the Independent Auditors Report states that

> *"In our opinion*
>
> - *The financial statements give a true and fair view of the state of the groups and of the parents companies affairs as of 29th May 2011"*

The overall aim of corporate governance is to ensure that the people, who run the company, do so for the good of the company and not for the personal gain of themselves.

Financial Strategy

Horizontal Analysis

For the second task of the assignment, the brief asks to formulate a financial strategy prepared from an analysis of the financial strengths and weaknesses of the organisation.

Money In £(m)	2011	2010	Difference	% Difference	+/-
Turnover	123,052	126,511	3,459	2.75	⬇
Operating Costs	81,975	82,839	864	1	⬇
Operating Profit	15,370	16,120	750	4.7	⬇
Operating Profit Margin	12.5%	12.75%	.25%	1.96	⬇

Figure 2 showing Horizontal analysis of Games Workshop Group plc. Source GWSG Annual Report, adapted by Dave Ray

The horizontal analysis of the annual report for the group has gone down in three elements of the table, with an overall average drop of 2.6%. However this could be attributed with the current recession and the fall of consumers spending, although the 2.6% is not as high as the overall average of the retail sector spending fall which was 3.5%[3.]

Operating costs have decreased by 1%, which is excellent in a climate where the majority of operating costs within most industries have increased. This consequently has had a knock on effect with the companies operating profit margin, which did fall, however the company controlling the costs of the business has only effected the profit margin fall of .25% maintaining the companies steady profit margin of 12% over the last three years

Key Financial Ratios

	2011	2010	Difference	+/-
Profitability ROCE	28.3%	28.2%	0.1%	⬆
Efficiency	2.3:1	2.2:1	.1	⬆
Liquidity	1.98:1	2:1	.02	⬇
Structure: Gearing	3.9%	3.5%	.4%	

Figure 3 showing the financial analysis of GWG adapted from annual report by Dave Ray

Profitability

The Return on Capital Employed refers to how well the company uses the investor's capital. So regarding Games Workshop Group plc, for every £1 invested by a shareholder, GWG will make a 28.3% (28.3p) return on the capital employed. Taking into consideration that a Shareholder invests in a company to possibly make a return on their investment, a 28.3% return compared to a shareholder investing their money in a high interest savings account or ISA of 4.5% interest is more financially rewarding. This section also shows that as a company, they are very effective in using capital and turning that into a profit.

Efficiency

The efficiency ratio for the company is strong, and improved by .1% compared to the previous year. The efficiency: Asset turnover ratio is a measure of how well a company uses its revenue, so looking at the efficiency ratio of GWG plc, in 2011 for every pound used in the business; the Games Workshop Group generated £1.30 in sales. For the business to improve on this statistic, the company could increase revenue by selling more or increasing the price of their products. However, increasing the price of the products may have a detrimental effect and reduce the turnover.

Liquidity

The liquidity: current ratio is the companies' ability to pay its way in the future. To summarise this area, if the business had to pay back all of its loans, could it do it, and how much money would it have left. So with the case of the GWG plc, at present it could pay all of its liabilities and still have money left as its ratio 1.98:1, which is a fall of .2% compared to the previous year. To improve this ratio the company could do any of the following in the table below

How do you remove excess cash?
• Pay back long term borrowing
• Buy back share capital
• Pay bigger dividends
• Buy fixed assets

Structure Gearing

The structure gearing of a company looks at the long term borrowing of a company, to interpret the GWG plc leverage ratio; in 2011 3.9% of the GWG plc assets were financed by borrowing. A figure that has gone up by .4% and this reflects the yellow in the table. It is not a majorly bad thing that it has gone up by .4% as this is very small, however it does show that the company does not have large long term borrowings, and if necessary if the company did need to generate capital it could do so from selling shares.

Proposed Strategy

Strategy has been defined in Rosenfeld et al (1999) as,

"the determination of the basic long-term goals and objectives of an enterprise and the adoption of courses of action and the allocation of resources necessary for carrying out these goals."

For developing a strategy, Ansoff (1957) developed the Product/Market Matrix which can be seen in figure 2 below

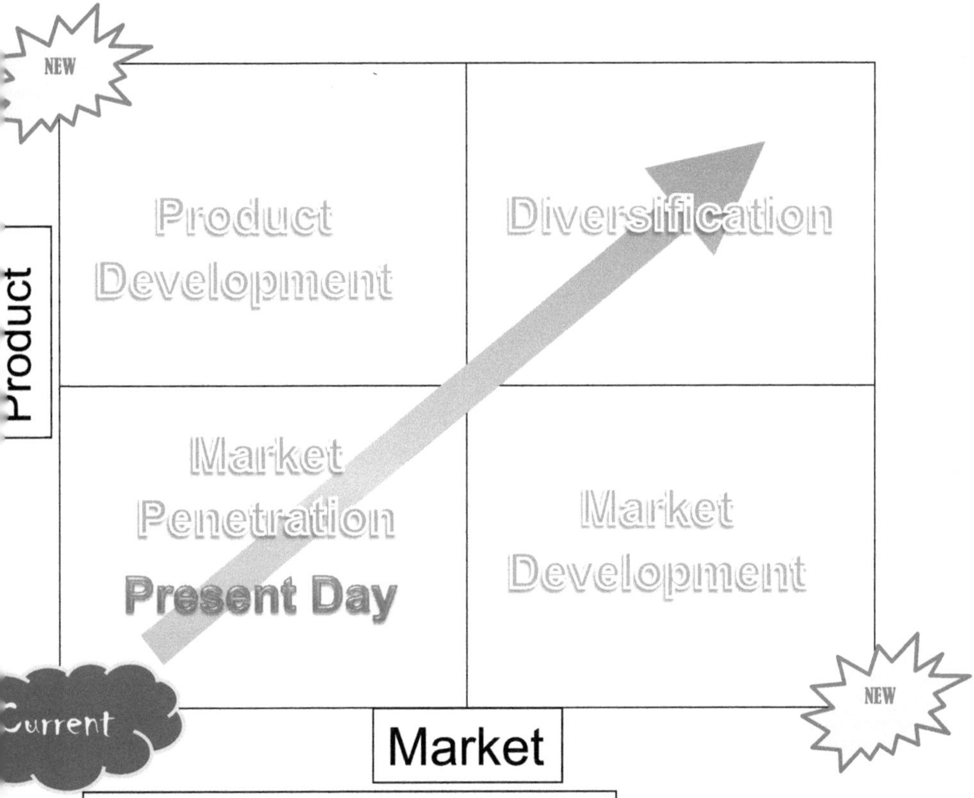

Figure 4 Showing Ansoff Matrix adapted by Dave Ray for Games Workshop

What is Ansoff's matrix? The Ansoff growth matrix assists organisations to map strategic product market growth by looking at the potential areas for growth.

Ansoff's Matrix can be explained in the table below.

<table>
<tr>
<td rowspan="2">Product</td>
<td>Product Development

Research and Development into New products</td>
<td>Diversification

Introducing New Products or services to the Customer
Kodak Cameras to Printers for example</td>
</tr>
<tr>
<td>Market Penetration

Firms try to increase market share by encouraging customers to buy more products</td>
<td>Market Development

A business will attempt to sell its products to new customers, possibly in new foreign markets</td>
</tr>
</table>

Fig 5 defining Ansoff Matrix: Adapted by Dave ray

Market

Referring back to Ansoff's matrix and regarding the company's annual report, the business has already got market domination in this area, and is developing new products to encourage their customers to keep spending their money with the company. Along with this the company has successfully entered foreign markets all over the world and have diversified into different markets with the company's publishing business which is thriving.

Proposing a financial strategy for a business that is underperforming is relatively easy in comparison to developing a strategy for a business that is doing well. It would be easy to suggest that a company should increase turnover and reduce costs, however a strategy such as this is already being implemented by the company, and is also stated in the annual report for the company that it should continue to increase turnover by introducing new customers to its business and at the same time control the costs within the business.

With this in mind the area that I feel that the company could expand is in the diversification part of Ansoff's Matrix, and the area that I believe that the company could expand into is the film industry. My reasons for suggesting this area is that the company already has a successful publishing company (The Black Library) and has many bestsellers. With these books come the rights for all plots and characters that are owned by the Games Workshop group, and I believe with these rights, and the network of writers, the company could surely create a film to be produced. Looking at The Games Workshops Groups competitor Hasbro Toys, they entered this market 25 years ago, first into children's cartoons, but more relevantly to the matter of films, in 2007 *Transformers* which grossed $709 million, 2009 *Revenge of the Fallen,* grossing $836 million and in 2011 *Dark of the Moon* grossed $1.12 billion, not to mention the cartoon film made in 1986 which grossed over $200 million. Along with this there are also the earnings that are made from merchandise, specifically toys, as well as the increased awareness of the toy products that specifically come from the films.

Having suggested the strategy of diversifying into the film industry, a strength, weakness, opportunity and weakness analysis has been created to provide an outlook of the idea

Strengths	Weakness
✓ Large Range of Characters ✓ Existing infrastructure of writing talent ✓ Own all of the trademarks and visual rights for characters ✓ Large international customer base ✓ Niche market that could be easily conveyed to unfamiliar audience range.	• No experience within the film Industry. • Large outlay of capital
Opportunities	Threats
• Increase Customer Base • Increase sales in merchandise • Increase in revenue for the company • Possibility of Sequels if film is successful	• The Film could be unsuccessful • Failure of film could incur damage to reputation to the business • Film may not recoup financial outlay incurred in making film

Figure 6 SWOT Analysis of proposed strategy

Concluding this section, I have reviewed the company's financial statements to find that the company has maintained a good level of profit margin while controlling its costs, however looking at The Games Workshop Groups competitor (as stated in datamonitor) Hasbro, the turnover for that company is $4.25 million, which equals to £2.6 million, which equates to 20% of GWG turnover. Other figures such as the profitability are 2% higher than GWG, which indicates that the Games Workshop Groups profit margins are similar to their competitor, but the structure gearing of Hasbro is significantly higher than GWG, which means Hasbro are depending more on long term borrowings.

Implementing Strategy

David (1995 p.5) writes that "the strategic-management process consists of three stages: Strategy formulation, strategy implementation, and strategy evaluation." With this in mind, the previous section of this report has looked at formulating a strategy and the following looks at ways a business implements its strategy

Before any plan is created or executed, a financial budget has to be created. A budget has been defined as *"An estimate of costs, revenues, and resources over a specified period, reflecting a reading of future financial conditions and goals."*[online] The budget has to be compatible with the long term strategy (which would be to remain solvent) but is based on a short term strategy (diversifying into a new market)

The most popular method of implementing a strategy is using Kaplan and Norton (1992) Balanced Scorecard. The Balanced Scorecard is used to **improve** the business's strategy and identify **key issues** that contribute to a better strategy.

So relating this to the Games Workshop Group plc, the strategy would be *"the business moving into a new market of film production to generate a new market, customer base and increase turnover."*

So applying Kaplan and Nortons Balanced Scorecard would look like figure 7

Figure 7 showing Kaplan and Norton Balanced Scorecard.

The balanced scorecard uses four key areas to help implement a company's strategy which can be seen in the table below

Financial	Customer
This area looks at the financial objectives of the company and allows the company to track financial success and shareholder value. The strategy for GWG is to increase turnover, and therefore increasing the shareholder return on investment	This section covers the customer objectives such as customer satisfaction, market share goals as well as products and services available to the customer The strategy relating to the customer aims at increasing its potential market share by diversifying into a different market and potentially attracting new customers while giving old customers something new.
Internal Business Process	Learning and Growth
This covers internal operational goals and outlines the key processes needed to deliver customer objectives This section would look at how the business needs to adapt in order to meet its strategic goals. For the business relating to its strategy, the business's process would have to be adapted to a new market.	This covers intangible drivers of future success, such as human capital and information capital including skills and training This relates to the company again having to look at what it needs to continue the success of the strategy, eg new employees with a different skill set for media marketing.

Source: http://www.ap-institute.com/Balanced%20Scorecard.html [online]

The balanced scorecard system of implementing strategy is used by a large amount of organisations, however this does not make it the best tool for implementing a company's strategy. Further research into the model reveals a few flaws that for me seem major flaws. Such flaws as that the balanced scorecard does not take into consideration any interest groups that could be related to the strategy (in the case of the GWC and the balanced scorecard could be Enthusiasts Clubs, Film critics etc) and also it does not take into account any competitors. A successful strategy also relies on knowing exactly what is happening in the external environment. . Simons et. al (2000, p. 58) recommends that it might be worthwhile to add a specific feature to every Balanced Scorecard where a team or a certain person will be assigned in every organisation who is directly responsible for collecting information about external opportunities and threats.

Personally I feel as if the balanced scorecard may be a useful tool on how to implement strategy, but it is not specific enough. Another model for implementing suggested by Speculand (2009) is the Instrumental Compass Model.

The Instrumental Compass is task specific and an example of this model is shown in figure 8

Figure 8; Instrumental Compass: Source, Speculand (2009)

The method has eight areas that need to be focused on to implement strategy effectively and is more organisation specific than the balanced scorecard. An example of this is that the balanced scorecard does not take into consideration a company's culture and how a new strategy may be affected by it, the Implementation Compass emphasis that a new strategy has an effect and that *"You must change the day-to-day activities of your staff members and have a culture that support and fosters change."* [online] For more information on the areas of the Implementation Compass see reference 4.

Once again though the Implementation Compass also has its weaknesses, the model does not take into consideration external factors like the balanced scorecard, and it does not take into consideration key stakeholder groups such as shareholder and customers. These two stakeholders are vital. The model does not take into consideration if the shareholders want to implement a new strategy or if customers would accept the end result of a new strategy.

I believe that if you were to use both the models for implementing a strategy, you would get the benefits of the balanced scorecards ability to strengthen the strategic planning and stakeholder's needs with the Implementation Compass's task specific list of organisational objectives. This leads to the following section of organisational structure.

Organisational Structure

> "Organisations have a formal structure which is the way that the organisation is organised by those with responsibility for managing the organisation. They create the formal structures that enable the organisation to meet its stated objectives." [online]

Wilson et al (1999) writes that "Structure is the established pattern of relationships between the component parts of an organisation, outlining communication, control and authority patterns." Relating this to the implementation of a strategy is that if the company creates a new strategy, does the company have the organisational structure to complete it, as well as being able to deal with the new systems, and communicating both the strategy and any issues throughout the organisation.

Conclusion

The report has looked at the company The Games Workshop Group plc and discussed the legal form of the business as well as its relationships with its stakeholders. The report then looked at the balance sheet of the company and analysed the figures from 2011, assessing the company's return on capital employed as well as the gearing and efficiency of the company assets. Following the assessment of the figures a strategy was developed that would improve the financial figures of the company, and a SWOT Analysis was done on the proposed strategy. The final part of the report looked at how this strategy was to be implemented and what models can be used to efficiently execute the strategy and how an organisations structure relates to the implementation of the strategy.

Before starting this module my knowledge in this area of corporate law was very limited, however associating a business to the theory has enabled me to expand on my knowledge as well as being able to assess a company's finances and create a theoretical strategy that could help the business. In reality I am aware that no business would take my strategy seriously as I have no previous experience in actually implementing any strategies, however by doing this module, I feel as if I was to be asked I would be confidently able to attempt it.

Bibliography

Books

Bové, C.L., and Thill, J.V (2005). Business in Action. 3rd ed. New Jersey: Pearson Prentice Hall

Clayton, P. (2008). *Forming a Limited Company (Business Development Series)*. 10th Edition. Kogan Page Ltd.

Dine, J. (1994). Company law. 2nd ed. London: Macmillan

Editors Of Perseus Publishing, (2002). *Business: The Ultimate Resource*. 1st Edition. Basic Books.

David, F R (1995). *Strategic Management*. 5th Edition. Prentice Hall.

Pride, William (2004). *Business 8th Edition*. 8 Edition. South-Western College Pub.

Rosenfeld, R. H., & Wilson D.C., (1999), Managing Organizations, 2nd edition. Berkshire: McCraw Hill

Simons, R. Dávila, A. (2000). Robert S Kaplan Performance Measurement & Control Systems for Implementing Strategy. Prentice Hall,

Speculand, R. (2009). *Beyond Strategy: The Leader's Role in Successful Implementation*. 1 Edition. Wiley.

Tricker, Bob (2003). *Essential Director*. Edition. Bloomberg Press.

Weetman, P. (2006). Financial and Management Accounting - 4th ed. - Harlow: Pearson Education Ltd

Wilson,D. (1998). *Managing Organizations*. 2nd Edition. McGraw-Hill Publishing Company.

Journal

Ansoff, I.: Strategies for Diversification, Harvard Business Review, Vol. 35 Issue 5,Sep-Oct 1957, pp. 113-124

Online Bibliography

Companies Act 2006. 2012. *Companies Act 2006*. [ONLINE] Available at: http://www.legislation.gov.uk/ukpga/2006/46/section/336. [Accessed 15 April 2012].

Requirements for public limited companies | Business Link . [ONLINE] Available at: http://www.businesslink.gov.uk/bdotg/action/detail?itemId=1085063937&r.i=1073789599&r.l

1=1073858805&r.l2=1085161962&r.l3=1073865436&r.t=RESOURCES&type=RESOURCE
S. [Accessed 15 April 2012].

Balanced Scorecard - explained: examples, templates and case studies. 2012. [ONLINE]
Available at: http://www.ap-institute.com/Balanced%20Scorecard.html. [Accessed 30 April
2012].

The Great Big Strategy Challenge. [ONLINE] Available at:
http://www.iqpc.com/redcontent.aspx?id=65786. [Accessed 30 April 2012].

The Times 100. 2012. *The formal and informal organisation structure Business organisation
business studies and business english | The Times 100.* [ONLINE] Available at:
http://www.thetimes100.co.uk/theory/theory--company--308.php. [Accessed 30 April 2012].

What is budget? definition and meaning. [ONLINE] Available at:
http://www.businessdictionary.com/definition/budget.html. [Accessed 30 April 2012].

Appendices

Reference 1

Dividend- A share of the after-tax profit of a company, distributed to its shareholders according to the number and class of shares held by them.

http://www.businessdictionary.com/definition/dividend.html#ixzz1s6eZXRHq

Reference 2

Stockholder - An individual, group, or organization that holds one or more shares in a company, and in whose name the share certificate is issued. Also called shareholder.

Read more: http://www.businessdictionary.com/definition/stockholder.html#ixzz1s6pMgg2g

Reference 3

The BRC-KPMG retail sales monitor showed that the total value of retail sales last month was 1.9% lower than in March 2010, but down 3.5% when the data was adjusted for an increase in floor space over the past 12 months.

Consumer spending hit by rise in inflation | Business | The Guardian . 2012. Available at: http://www.guardian.co.uk/business/2011/apr/12/consumer-spending-inflation. [Accessed 17 April 2012].

Refernce 4

1. People

It is not leadership that implements strategy but people

Questions to consider:

Do you have the right caliber of people? Do they have the competencies to execute the new strategy? Are they motivated to do so?

2. Biz Case

The emotional and numerical rational for adopting the strategy

Questions to consider: Why is the strategy center stage? Do your staff members know what to do differently on the Monday morning after implementation is announced? Do they have the right tools and techniques to implement the strategy?

3. Communication

People can only adopt a strategy if they know about it and understand it

Questions to consider: Do all your staff know what the new strategy is and why it has been adopted? Is the strategy communicated in a way that it comes alive?

4. Measurement

"You must inspect what you expect." Have the right measures in place

Questions to consider: Do you have the right measures for the new strategy? Are the measures being leveraged to guide the implementation?

5. Culture

You must change the day-to-day activities of your staff members and have a culture that support and fosters change

Questions to consider: What needs to change in the fundamental way you are working so as to encourage the adoption of the new culture? Are we using the language of the new strategy?

6. Process

There must be congruence between what you say you are going to do (strategy implementation) and what you are doing (the process)

Questions to consider: Do your processes support or hinder the new strategy? Where can you redesign the process so it is more supportive and effective?

7. Reinforcement

You must reinforce the expected behaviors so that they are continuously repeated

Questions to consider: When staff members step in to the unknown and demonstrate the new behaviors, are they recognized and rewarded? Does the reinforcement encourage them to continue to demonstrate the desired new behaviors?

8. Review

The weakest of the eight points among leaders - you must constantly review to make sure the right actions are being taken to deliver the right results

The Games Workshop Group Plc

Horizontal Analysis

	A	B	A-B	(Difference / B) x 100
	Current Year	**Previous Year**	**Difference**	**Percentage Difference**
Turnover a.k.a. Revenue from continuing operations	123.052	126,511	-3,459	-2.75%
Operating costs	81,975	82,839	864	-1%
Operating profit a.k.a. Profit on operations OR Profit from continuing operations	15,370	16,120	-750	-4.7
Operating profit margin Operating profit x 100 Turnover	12.5%	12.75%	-.25%	-1.96%

The Games Workshop Group Plc

Financial Analysis

Key Financial Ratios

Note: see overleaf regarding different definitions under UK GAAP and IAS *e.g.* turnover (UK GAAP) may be referred to as Revenue from continuing operations. Long term borrowing (for the Gearing calculation) can be found on the Balance Sheet under Non-Current Liabilities.

	A Current Year	B Previous Year	B - A Difference
Profitability: Return on capital employed Operating profit (from P&L) Total assets less current liabilities (from balance sheet) x 100	28.3%	28.2%	.1%
Efficiency: Asset turnover Turnover (from P&L) Total assets less current liabilities	2.3:1	2.2:1	.1
Liquidity: Current ratio See balance sheet for both Current assets Current liabilities	1.98:1	2:1	-.02
Structure: Gearing Both figures can be found on the balance sheet Long term borrowing Total assets less current liabilities x 100	3.9%	3.5%	.4%

Hasbro Plc

Horizontal Analysis

	A	B	A-B	(Difference / B) x 100
	Current Year	Previous Year	Difference	Percentage Difference
Turnover a.k.a. Revenue from continuing operations	4.25	4.02	12	-3.0
Operating costs	3.7	3.4	.3	8.8
Operating profit a.k.a. Profit on operations OR Profit from continuing operations	.595	.587	-97.9	-13.81
Operating profit margin Operating profit x 100 / Turnover	14%	14.6%	.6%	-4.1%

Hasbro Plc

Financial Analysis

Key Financial Ratios

Note: see overleaf regarding different definitions under UK GAAP and IAS *e.g.* turnover (UK GAAP) may be referred to as Revenue from continuing operations. Long term borrowing (for the Gearing calculation) can be found on the Balance Sheet under Non-Current Liabilities.

	A	B	B - A
	Current Year	Previous Year	Difference
Profitability: Return on capital employed			
Operating profit (from P&L) Total assets less current liabilities (from balance sheet) x 100	45%	39%	6%
Efficiency: Asset turnover			
Turnover (from P&L) Total assets less current liabilities	1:3.25	1:2.7	.55
Liquidity: Current ratio See balance sheet for both	1:2.3	1:3.1	-.8
Current assets Current liabilities			
Structure: Gearing Both figures can be found on the balance sheet			
Long term borrowing Total assets less current liabilities x 100	45%	42%	3%